I0797366

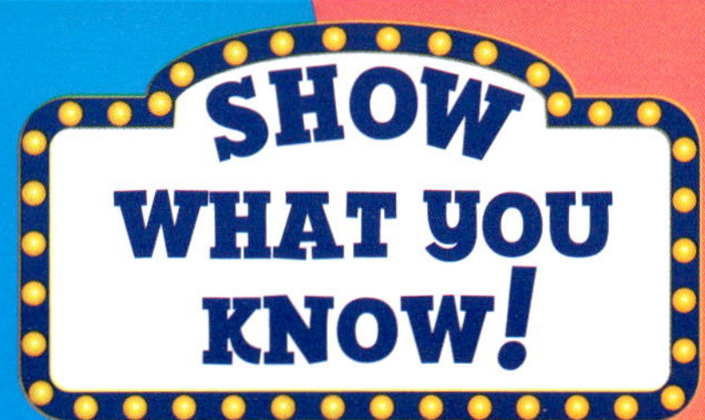

Creating and Sharing a Slide Show

by Ann Truesdell

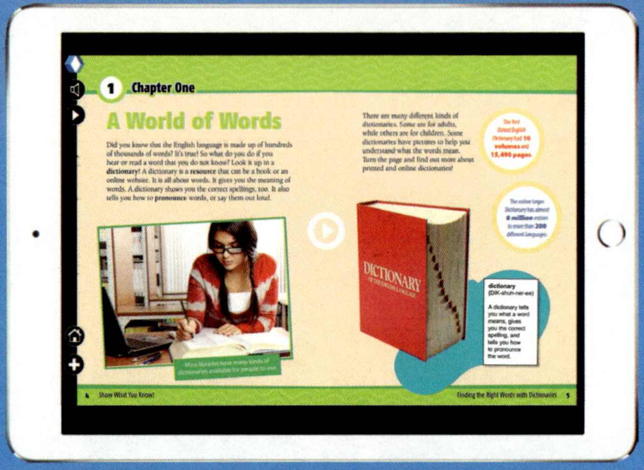

Lightbox is an all-inclusive digital solution for the teaching and learning of curriculum topics in an original, groundbreaking way. Lightbox is based on National Curriculum Standards.

STANDARD FEATURES OF LIGHTBOX

AUDIO High-quality narration using text-to-speech system

ACTIVITIES Printable PDFs that can be emailed and graded

SLIDESHOWS Pictorial overviews of key concepts

VIDEOS Embedded high-definition video clips

WEBLINKS Curated links to external, child-safe resources

TRANSPARENCIES Step-by-step layering of maps, diagrams, charts, and timelines

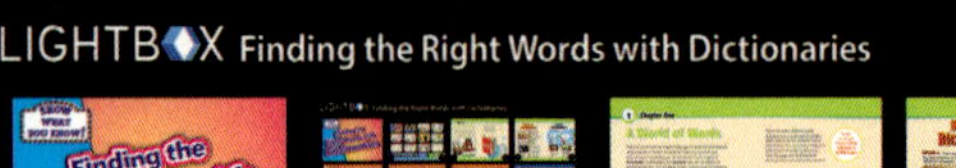

INTERACTIVE MAPS Interactive maps and aerial satellite imagery

QUIZZES Ten multiple choice questions that are automatically graded and emailed for teacher assessment

KEY WORDS Matching key concepts to their definitions

Creating and Sharing a Slide Show

1 Chapter One

Share with a Slide Show

Eddy's teacher has asked him to create a presentation about tigers for the class. He is excited! He will speak in front of everyone. He will also have a slide show to share! A slide show displays a series of screens called slides. Slides use pictures, words, videos, music, or graphs as **visual aids**. They help the audience understand what the presenter is talking about.

People in business use slide shows to share their ideas. Teachers use them to teach students new information. Students can use slide shows to show what they have learned. You can make a slide show on almost any computer. When it is time to give a presentation, you can connect the computer to a projector or a video screen. Then everyone can see your slides!

Prezi has more than **85 million users** worldwide.

There are many computer programs you can use to create a slide show. Microsoft PowerPoint and Apple Keynote are two of the most widely used slide show programs. There are also websites that let you create presentations online. These sites include Prezi, SlideShare, Zoho Show, Empressr, and Prezentit. Finally, there are many slide show apps that you can use on tablet computers. Ask an adult to help you access a slide show program on a computer or other device. Try it out! What can you create for fun?

On any day, more than **35 million PowerPoint presentations** are being given.

History of Slide Shows

1659
The magic lantern is invented. It allows pictures painted on glass to be shone onto walls.

Late 1700s
The magic lantern is used in theaters as entertainment.

1800s
Magic lanterns are used during classes and storytelling sessions.

1848
Photographs are put on glass, replacing the painted pictures.

1935
Kodachrome film is invented. Pictures can now be put on small plates, called slides, and shown using slide projectors.

1950s
People begin developing slide shows for home use.

1980s
The digital slide show is created.

Mapping Slide Shows

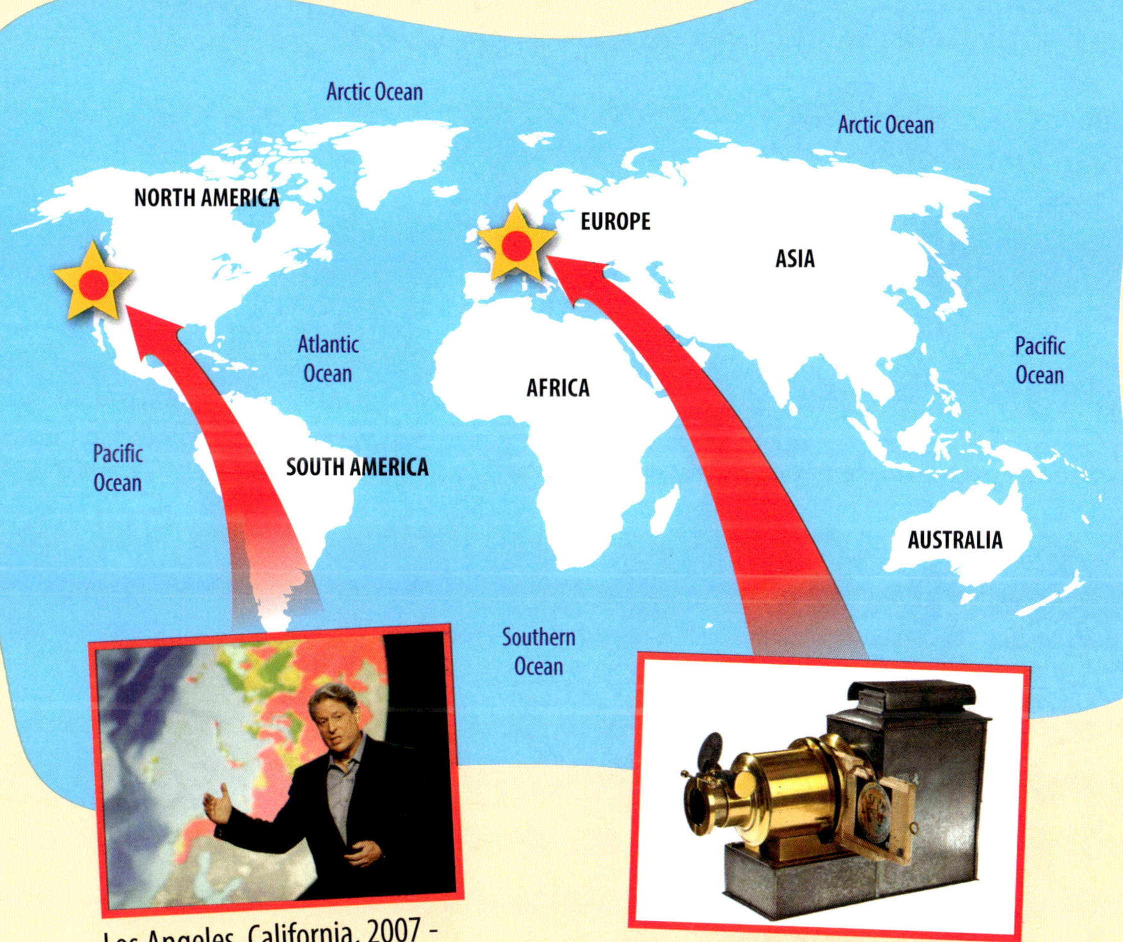

Los Angeles, California, 2007 - *An Inconvenient Truth*, a movie based on Vice President Al Gore's "most famous slide show in the world", about climate change, wins two Academy Awards.

The Hague, Netherlands, 1659 - Scientist Christiaan Huygens invents the magic lantern.

2 Chapter Two

Just the Facts

Eddy reads about his topic in books. He also looks for information on the Internet. Then he organizes all of his facts into a slide show.

Make sure slide show information is organized, not random.

Presentations have a beginning, middle, and end. This makes it easier for the audience to follow what the presenter is talking about. Eddy starts with the basics. He discusses what tigers look like and where they live. Eddy adds more specific details in the middle of his presentation. He describes how tigers live. He also poses a problem: tigers may die out soon. At the end of his slide show, Eddy wraps things up. He explains what the audience can do to save tigers.

At first, Eddy plans to include a whole paragraph on a slide. But his sister says it looks boring. There's too much text for his audience to read. Eddy's dad suggests breaking the text into short bullet points instead. Bullet points are small dots that show different ideas in a list. Each bullet point is followed by a few words or a short sentence.

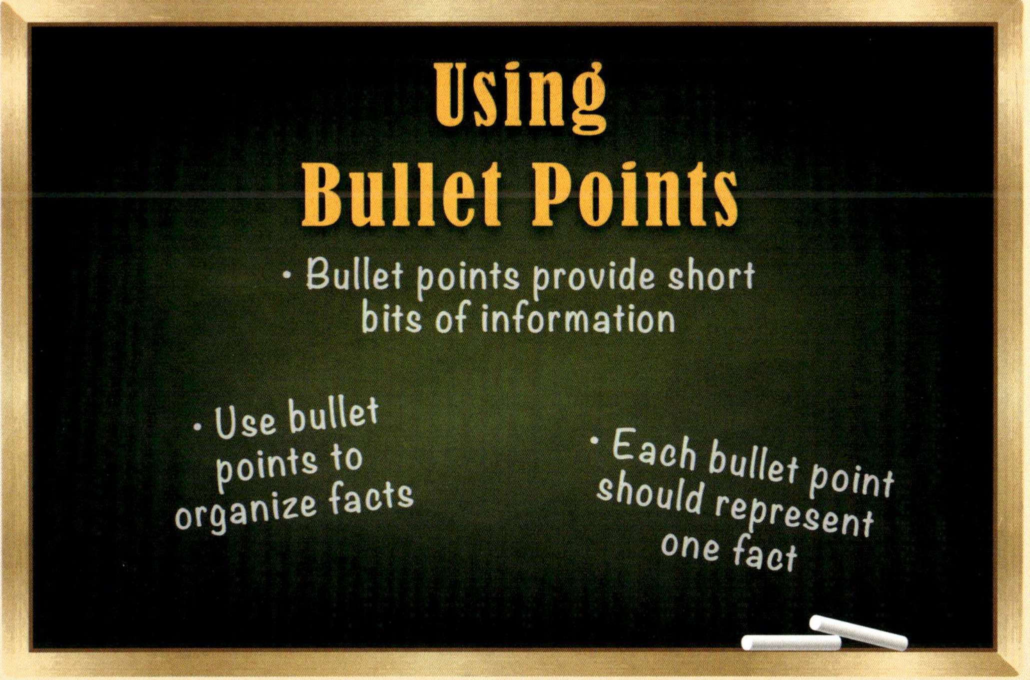

Try This

The order of your slides is very important. If you present information out of order, your audience might be confused.

Imagine you are helping Eddy prepare his presentation. You have created four slides with facts. The title of each slide is listed below. Which order would you put them in? Why?

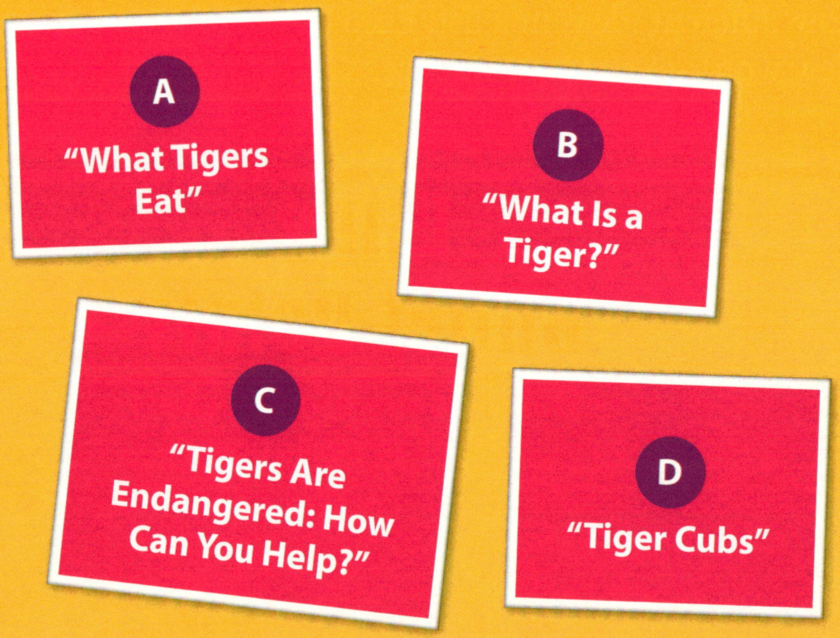

Answers: You might order your slides like this: B, A, D, C.
Another possible order might be B, D, A, C.

Slide B comes first because it gives background information to your audience about what a tiger is. Slides D and A come next. They help you tell your story by giving further information about tigers. You end with slide C because it will leave your audience thinking about what they can do to help tigers.

Make sure the order of your slides makes sense.

3 Chapter Three

Show Off Your Stripes

Slide show presentations need more than just words. Putting pictures on a presentation's slides will keep an audience interested. Pictures can also make a presentation easier to understand.

Photos can make your presentation more interesting and informative.

You can use photos to help explain different parts of your topic.

Images should add important information to a presentation. For example, Eddy's presentation includes a slide about tiger cubs. He adds a photo of a tiger cub to that slide to show his audience what a cub looks like.

Not all images are helpful. Many presentation programs come with built-in clip art. Clip art is usually made up of cartoonish drawings. A clip art picture of a tiger is not as useful as a photograph of a real tiger! It doesn't give the audience any useful information about tigers.

Map of Tiger Populations

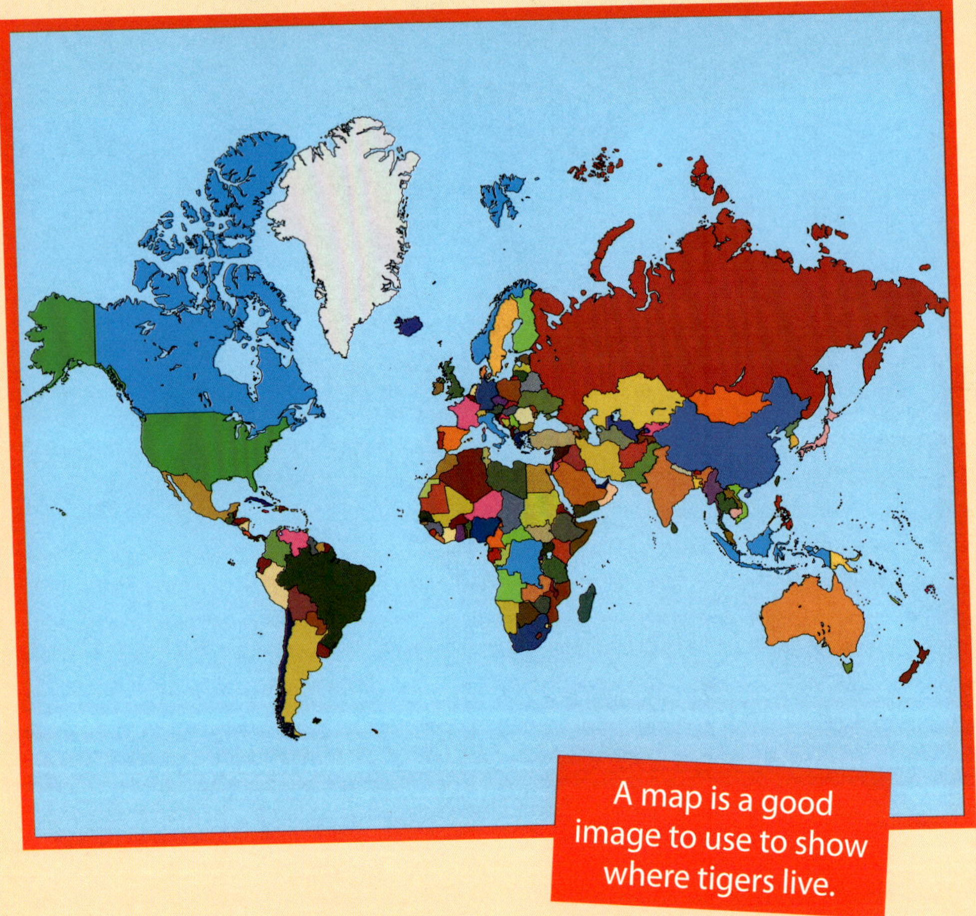

A map is a good image to use to show where tigers live.

Animated clip art, such as a cartoon tiger running, is not helpful either. However, Eddy does want to show a tiger in action. He decides to **embed** a video of a running tiger in his presentation. Short videos can make a presentation very interesting! In some cases, such as showing how a tiger moves, a video clip would be a better choice than a picture.

Graphs, charts, timelines, and maps can also be added to a presentation. Eddy gives credit to where he found each picture, video, or other visual aid.

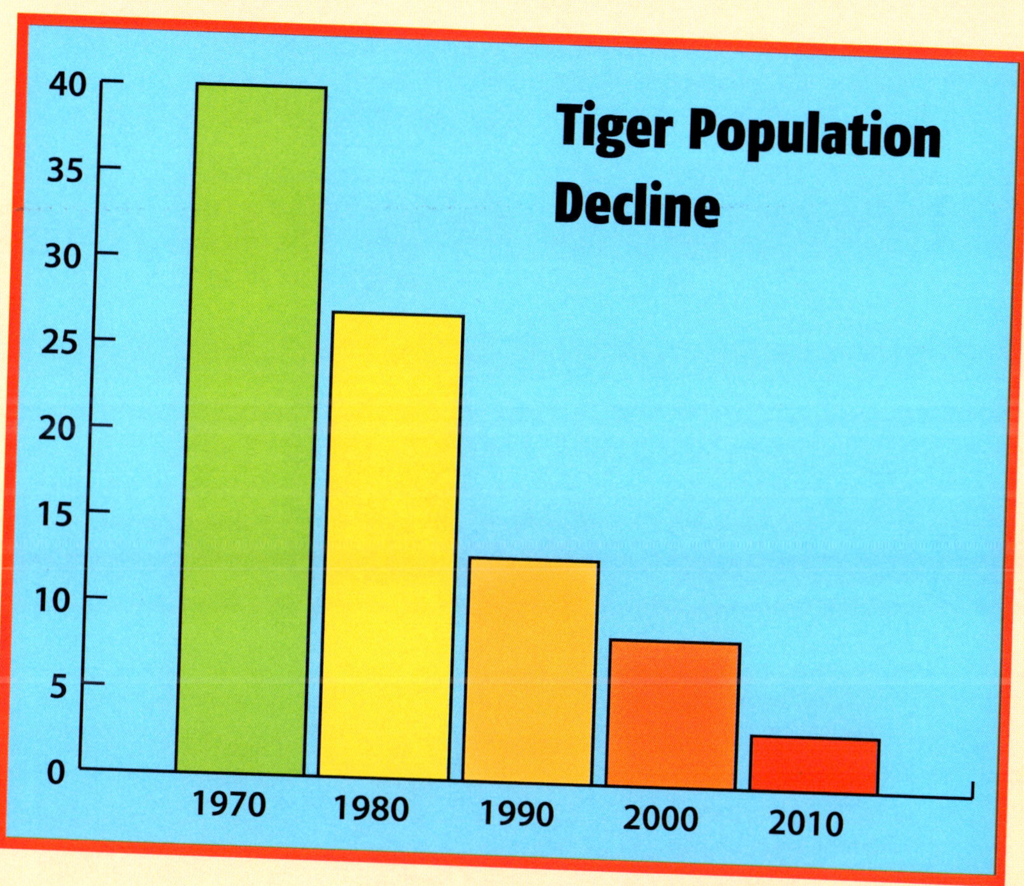

Graphs are a great way to show information that includes numbers.

Try This

Let's add images to Eddy's slide show. Look at the slide titles and images below. Which pictures belong on which slides?

SLIDES

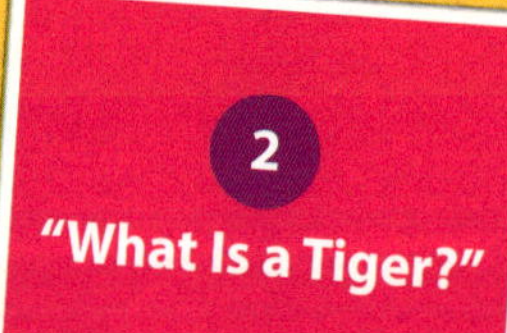

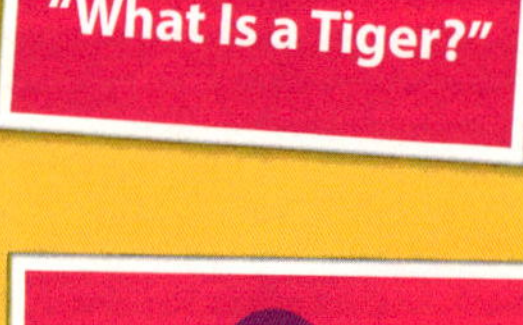

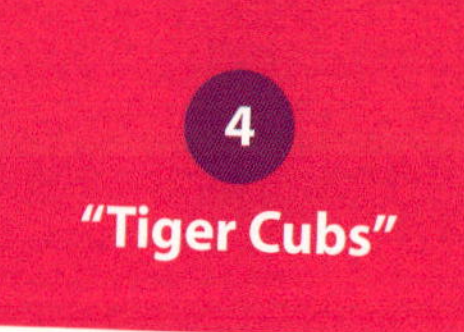

PICTURES

Picture of a tiger cub

Picture of an adult tiger

Picture of a deer or wild pig

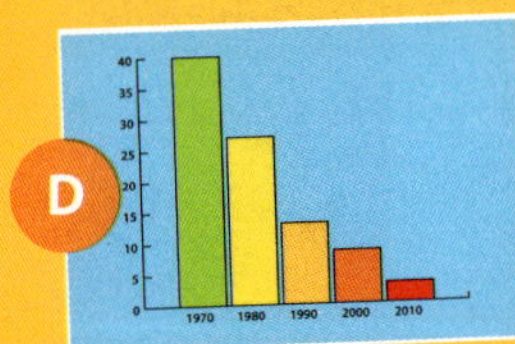

Graph showing the decline in the tiger population

Answers: 1-C, 2-B, 3-D, 4-A

4 Chapter Three

Make It Shine

It is finally time for Eddy to design his presentation. This means choosing **fonts** and colors. He also needs to decide how to organize the different slides. The design should make it easy to see the words and images on the slides.

Eddy wants to choose fonts that are easy to read. First, he tries a cursive font. But when he shows the slides to his mom, she has trouble reading the text. Fancy fonts look pretty, but are harder to read. Very basic fonts are clearer. Eddy's dad suggests he use Verdana, Arial, or Times New Roman.

Eddy also needs the text to be big enough for everyone to see, no matter where they sit. Font sizes from 18 to 24 points are usually good for presentations.

Certain fonts are easier to read than others.

Some backgrounds can be distracting.

There are **more than 90,000 fonts**.

Eddy tries different backgrounds for his slides. He finds that solid-colored backgrounds that are not too bright work best. Very bright colors make it hard to read the words on the slides. Text should stick out against the background color. This is called **contrast**. A light-colored background and dark text is a great contrast. A dark background with light text also works. Eddy chooses a dark green background and pale yellow text.

Helvetica is the **most widely used font** in print.

Next, Eddy designs each slide's layout. He tries different ways of organizing text and images. The computer program he uses came with some **template**s to help him. He finds that three to five bullet points per slide works best. He only includes one or two pictures on each slide. He tried fitting more, but it looked too crowded.

Finally, Eddy adds a title to each slide to tell what the slide is about. The title font is bigger than the font used for the bullet points. He shows the finished presentation to his family. They love it!

Quiz

1
What are two computer programs that people can use to create a slide show?

2
Who invented the magic lantern?

3
What are bullet points?

4
How do pictures help a slide show?

5
What type of information can be shown in a graph?

6
What are three basic fonts that can be used in slide shows?

7
What size of font is good for presentations?

8
How many fonts are there?

9
What is contrast?

10
Should a title font be bigger or smaller than the font used for bullet points?

Answers: 1. Microsoft PowerPoint and Apple Keynote **2.** Christiaan Huygens **3.** Small dots that show different ideas in a list **4.** They keep the audience interested and make the presentation easier to understand. **5.** Information that includes numbers **6.** Verdana, Arial, and Times New Roman **7.** 18 to 24 points **8.** More than 90,000 **9.** When text sticks out against a background color. **10.** Bigger

Key Words

contrast: the difference between two things

embed: to make something a part of something else, such as placing a video file into a slide show presentation

fonts: styles of text

templates: documents or patterns that are used to create similar documents

visual aids: things people can look at to help them understand ideas and facts in a presentation

Index

LIGHTBOX

SUPPLEMENTARY RESOURCES

Click on the plus icon found in the bottom left corner of each spread to open additional teacher resources.

- Download and print the book's quizzes and activities
- Access curriculum correlations
- Explore additional web applications that enhance the Lightbox experience

LIGHTBOX DIGITAL TITLES

Packed full of integrated media

VIDEOS

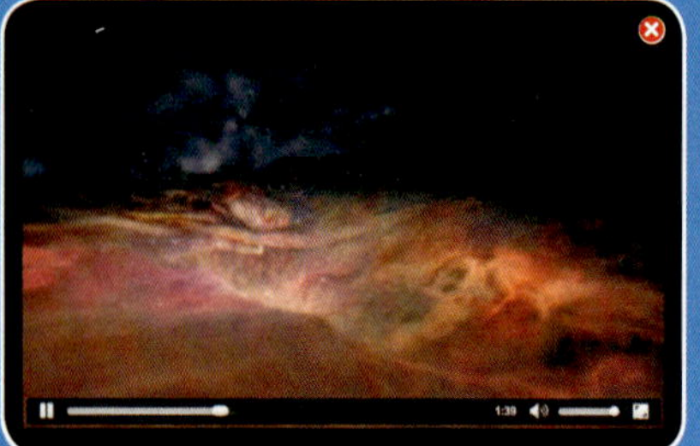

INTERACTIVE MAPS

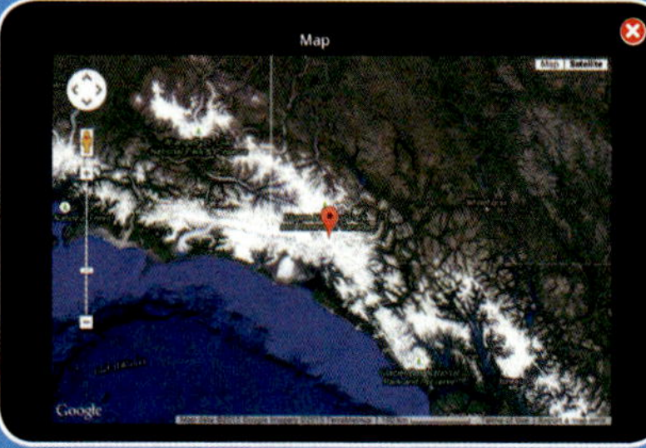

WEBLINKS

SLIDESHOWS

A cirque is a rounded, bowl-shaped area where snow collects.

QUIZZES

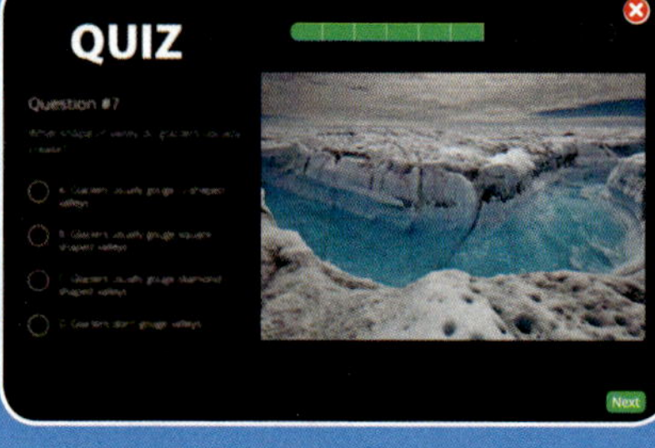

OPTIMIZED FOR

- ✓ TABLETS
- ✓ WHITEBOARDS
- ✓ COMPUTERS
- ✓ AND MUCH MORE!

Published by Smartbook Media Inc.
350 5th Avenue, 59th Floor
New York, NY 10118
Website: www.openlightbox.com

First published by Cherry Lake Publishing in 2013

Library of Congress Control Number: 2018941474

ISBN 978-1-5105-3981-5 (hardcover)
ISBN 978-1-5105-3982-2 (multi-user eBook)

Printed in Brainerd, Minnesota, United States
1 2 3 4 5 6 7 8 9 0 22 21 20 19 18

062018
120517

Project Coordinator Heather Kissock
Designer Nick Newton

Photo Credits
Every reasonable effort has been made to trace ownership and to obtain permission to reprint copyright material. The publisher would be pleased to have any errors or omissions brought to its attention so that they may be corrected in subsequent printings.

The publisher acknowledges Getty Images, Shutterstock, Alamy, and iStock as its primary image suppliers for this title.